A SHROPSHIRE LAD

AND

LAST POEMS

By A. E. HOUSMAN

A Shropshire Lad and Last Poems
By A. E. Housman

Print ISBN 13: 978-1-4209-6653-4
eBook ISBN 13: 978-1-4209-6654-1

This edition copyright © 2020. Digireads.com Publishing.

All rights reserved. No part of this publication may be reproduced, distributed, or transmitted in any form or by any means, including photocopying, recording, or other electronic or mechanical methods, without the prior written permission of the publisher, except in the case of brief quotations embodied in critical reviews and certain other noncommercial uses permitted by copyright law.

Cover Image: a detail of an illustration by William Hyde, which appeared in the 1908 illustrated edition of *A Shropshire Lad*, published by Grant Richards Ltd., London.

Please visit *www.digireads.com*

CONTENTS

A SHROPSHIRE LAD 5

LAST POEMS 48

I

1887

From Clee to heaven the beacon burns,
    The shires have seen it plain,
From north and south the sign returns
    And beacons burn again.

Look left, look right, the hills are bright,
    The dales are light between,
Because 'tis fifty years to-night
    That God has saved the Queen.

Now, when the flame they watch not towers
    About the soil they trod,
Lads, we'll remember friends of ours
    Who shared the work with God.

To skies that knit their heartstrings right,
    To fields that bred them brave,
The saviours come not home to-night:
    Themselves they could not save.

It dawns in Asia, tombstones show
    And Shropshire names are read;
And the Nile spills his overflow
    Beside the Severn's dead.

We pledge in peace by farm and town
    The Queen they served in war,
And fire the beacons up and down
    The land they perished for.

"God Save the Queen" we living sing,
    From height to height 'tis heard;
And with the rest your voices ring,
    Lads of the Fifty-third.

Oh, God will save her, fear you not:
    Be you the men you've been,
Get you the sons your fathers got,
    And God will Save the Queen.

II

Loveliest of trees, the cherry now
Is hung with bloom along the bough,
And stands about the woodland ride
Wearing white for Eastertide.

Now, of my threescore years and ten,
Twenty will not come again,
And take from seventy springs a score,
It only leaves me fifty more.

And since to look at things in bloom
Fifty springs are little room,
About the woodlands I will go
To see the cherry hung with snow.

III

THE RECRUIT

Leave your home behind, lad,
    And reach your friends your hand,
And go, and luck go with you
    While Ludlow tower shall stand.

Oh, come you home of Sunday
    When Ludlow streets are still
And Ludlow bells are calling
    To farm and lane and mill,

Or come you home of Monday
    When Ludlow market hums
And Ludlow chimes are playing
    "The conquering hero comes,"

Come you home a hero,
    Or come not home at all,
The lads you leave will mind you
    Till Ludlow tower shall fall.

And you will list the bugle
    That blows in lands of morn,
And make the foes of England
    Be sorry you were born.

And you till trump of doomsday
    On lands of morn may lie,
And make the hearts of comrades
    Be heavy where you die.

Leave your home behind you,
    Your friends by field and town
Oh, town and field will mind you
    Till Ludlow tower is down.

IV

REVEILLE

Wake: the silver dusk returning
    Up the beach of darkness brims,
And the ship of sunrise burning
    Strands upon the eastern rims.

Wake: the vaulted shadow shatters,
    Trampled to the floor it spanned,
And the tent of night in tatters
    Straws the sky-pavilioned land.

Up, lad, up, 'tis late for lying:
    Hear the drums of morning play;
Hark, the empty highways crying
    "Who'll beyond the hills away?"

Towns and countries woo together,
    Forelands beacon, belfries call;
Never lad that trod on leather
    Lived to feast his heart with all.

Up, lad: thews that lie and cumber
    Sunlit pallets never thrive;
Morns abed and daylight slumber
    Were not meant for man alive.

Clay lies still, but blood's a rover;
    Breath's a ware that will not keep
Up, lad: when the journey's over
    There'll be time enough to sleep.

V

Oh see how thick the goldcup flowers
    Are lying in field and lane,
With dandelions to tell the hours
    That never are told again.
Oh may I squire you round the meads
    And pick you posies gay?
—'Twill do no harm to take my arm.
    "You may, young man, you may."

Ah, spring was sent for lass and lad,
    'Tis now the blood runs gold,
And man and maid had best be glad
    Before the world is old.
What flowers to-day may flower to-morrow,
    But never as good as new.
—Suppose I wound my arm right round—
    "'Tis true, young man, 'tis true."

Some lads there are, 'tis shame to say,
    That only court to thieve,
And once they bear the bloom away
    'Tis little enough they leave.
Then keep your heart for men like me
    And safe from trustless chaps.
My love is true and all for you.
    "Perhaps, young man, perhaps."

Oh, look in my eyes, then, can you doubt?
    —Why, 'tis a mile from town.
How green the grass is all about!
    We might as well sit down.
—Ah, life, what is it but a flower?
    Why must true lovers sigh?
Be kind, have pity, my own, my pretty,—
    "Good-bye, young man, good-bye."

VI

When the lad for longing sighs,
    Mute and dull of cheer and pale,
If at death's own door he lies,
    Maiden, you can heal his ail.

Lovers' ills are all to buy:
    The wan look, the hollow tone,
The hung head, the sunken eye,
    You can have them for your own.

Buy them, buy them: eve and morn
    Lovers' ills are all to sell.
Then you can lie down forlorn;
    But the lover will be well.

VII

When smoke stood up from Ludlow,
    And mist blew off from Teme,
And blithe afield to ploughing
    Against the morning beam
    I strode beside my team,

The blackbird in the coppice
    Looked out to see me stride,
And hearkened as I whistled
    The tramping team beside,
    And fluted and replied:

"Lie down, lie down, young yeoman;
    What use to rise and rise?
Rise man a thousand mornings
    Yet down at last he lies,
    And then the man is wise."

I heard the tune he sang me,
    And spied his yellow bill;
I picked a stone and aimed it
    And threw it with a will:
    Then the bird was still.

Then my soul within me
    Took up the blackbird's strain,
And still beside the horses
    Along the dewy lane
    It sang the song again:

"Lie down, lie down, young yeoman;
    The sun moves always west;
The road one treads to labour
    Will lead one home to rest,
    And that will be the best."

VIII

"Farewell to barn and stack and tree,
    Farewell to Severn shore.
Terence, look your last at me,
    For I come home no more.

"The sun burns on the half-mown hill,
    By now the blood is dried;
And Maurice amongst the hay lies still
    And my knife is in his side."

"My mother thinks us long away;
    'Tis time the field were mown.
She had two sons at rising day,
    To-night she'll be alone."

"And here's a bloody hand to shake,
    And oh, man, here's good-bye;
We'll sweat no more on scythe and rake,
    My bloody hands and I."

"I wish you strength to bring you pride,
    And a love to keep you clean,
And I wish you luck, come Lammastide,
    At racing on the green."

"Long for me the rick will wait,
    And long will wait the fold,
And long will stand the empty plate,
    And dinner will be cold."

IX

On moonlit heath and lonesome bank
    The sheep beside me graze;
And yon the gallows used to clank
    Fast by the four cross ways.

A careless shepherd once would keep
    The flocks by moonlight there,[1]
And high amongst the glimmering sheep
    The dead man stood on air.

They hang us now in Shrewsbury jail:
    The whistles blow forlorn,
And trains all night groan on the rail
    To men that die at morn.

There sleeps in Shrewsbury jail to-night,
    Or wakes, as may betide,
A better lad, if things went right,
    Than most that sleep outside.

And naked to the hangman's noose
    The morning clocks will ring
A neck God made for other use
    Than strangling in a string.

And sharp the link of life will snap,
    And dead on air will stand
Heels that held up as straight a chap
    As treads upon the land.

So here I'll watch the night and wait
    To see the morning shine,
When he will hear the stroke of eight
    And not the stroke of nine;

And wish my friend as sound a sleep
    As lads' I did not know,
That shepherded the moonlit sheep
    A hundred years ago.

---

[1] Hanging in chains was called keeping sheep by moonlight.

X

MARCH

The Sun at noon to higher air,
Unharnessing the silver Pair
That late before his chariot swam,
Rides on the gold wool of the Ram.

So braver notes the storm-cock sings
To start the rusted wheel of things,
And brutes in field and brutes in pen
Leap that the world goes round again.

The boys are up the woods with day
To fetch the daffodils away,
And home at noonday from the hills
They bring no dearth of daffodils.

Afield for palms the girls repair,
And sure enough the palms are there,
And each will find by hedge or pond
Her waving silver-tufted wand.

In farm and field through all the shire
The eye beholds the heart's desire;
Ah, let not only mine be vain,
For lovers should be loved again.

XI

On your midnight pallet lying
    Listen, and undo the door:
Lads that waste the light in sighing
    In the dark should sigh no more;
Night should ease a lover's sorrow;
    Therefore, since I go to-morrow;
Pity me before.

In the land to which I travel,
    The far dwelling, let me say—
Once, if here the couch is gravel,
    In a kinder bed I lay,
And the breast the darnel smothers

    Rested once upon another's
        When it was not clay.

XII

When I watch the living meet,
    And the moving pageant file
Warm and breathing through the street
    Where I lodge a little while,

If the heats of hate and lust
    In the house of flesh are strong,
Let me mind the house of dust
    Where my sojourn shall be long.

In the nation that is not
    Nothing stands that stood before;
There revenges are forgot,
    And the hater hates no more;

Lovers lying two and two
    Ask not whom they sleep beside,
And the bridegroom all night through
    Never turns him to the bride.

XIII

When I was one-and-twenty
    I heard a wise man say,
"Give crowns and pounds and guineas
    But not your heart away;
Give pearls away and rubies
    But keep your fancy free."
But I was one-and-twenty,
    No use to talk to me.

When I was one-and-twenty
    I heard him say again,
"The heart out of the bosom
    Was never given in vain;
'Tis paid with sighs a plenty
    And sold for endless rue."
And I am two-and-twenty,
    And oh, 'tis true, 'tis true.

XIV

There pass the careless people
    That call their souls their own:
Here by the road I loiter,
    How idle and alone.

Ah, past the plunge of plummet,
    In seas I cannot sound,
My heart and soul and senses,
    World without end, are drowned.

His folly has not fellow
    Beneath the blue of day
That gives to man or woman
    His heart and soul away.

There flowers no balm to sain him
    From east of earth to west
That's lost for everlasting
    The heart out of his breast.

Here by the labouring highway
    With empty hands I stroll:
Sea-deep, till doomsday morning,
    Lie lost my heart and soul.

XV

Look not in my eyes, for fear
    They mirror true the sight I see,
And there you find your face too clear
    And love it and be lost like me.
One the long nights through must lie
    Spent in star-defeated sighs,
But why should you as well as I
    Perish? gaze not in my eyes.

A Grecian lad, as I hear tell,
    One that many loved in vain,
Looked into a forest well
    And never looked away again.
There, when the turf in springtime flowers,
    With downward eye and gazes sad,

    Stands amid the glancing showers
        A jonquil, not a Grecian lad.

XVI

    It nods and curtseys and recovers
        When the wind blows above,
    The nettle on the graves of lovers
        That hanged themselves for love.

    The nettle nods, the wind blows over,
        The man, he does not move,
    The lover of the grave, the lover
        That hanged himself for love.

XVII

    Twice a week the winter thorough
        Here stood I to keep the goal:
    Football then was fighting sorrow
        For the young man's soul.

    Now in May time to the wicket
        Out I march with bat and pad:
    See the son of grief at cricket
        Trying to be glad.

    Try I will; no harm in trying:
        Wonder 'tis how little mirth
    Keeps the bones of man from lying
        On the bed of earth.

XVIII

    Oh, when I was in love with you,
        Then I was clean and brave,
    And miles around the wonder grew
        How well did I behave.

    And now the fancy passes by,
        And nothing will remain,
    And miles around they'll say that I
        Am quite myself again.

XIX

TO AN ATHLETE DYING YOUNG

The time you won your town the race
We chaired you through the market-place;
Man and boy stood cheering by,
And home we brought you shoulder-high.

To-day, the road all runners come,
Shoulder-high we bring you home,
And set you at your threshold down,
Townsman of a stiller town.

Smart lad, to slip betimes away
From fields where glory does not stay
And early though the laurel grows
It withers quicker than the rose.

Eyes the shady night has shut
Cannot see the record cut,
And silence sounds no worse than cheers
After earth has stopped the ears:

Now you will not swell the rout
Of lads that wore their honours out,
Runners whom renown outran
And the name died before the man.

So set, before its echoes fade,
The fleet foot on the sill of shade,
And hold to the low lintel up
The still-defended challenge-cup.

And round that early-laurelled head
Will flock to gaze the strengthless dead,
And find unwithered on its curls
The garland briefer than a girl's.

XX

Oh fair enough are sky and plain,
    But I know fairer far:
Those are as beautiful again
    That in the water are;

The pools and rivers wash so clean
    The trees and clouds and air,
The like on earth was never seen,
    And oh that I were there.

These are the thoughts I often think
    As I stand gazing down
In act upon the cressy brink
    To strip and dive and drown;

But in the golden-sanded brooks
    And azure meres I spy
A silly lad that longs and looks
    And wishes he were I.

XXI

BREDON HILL[2]

In summertime on Bredon
    The bells they sound so clear;
Round both the shires they ring them
    In steeples far and near,
    A happy noise to hear.

Here of a Sunday morning
    My love and I would lie
And see the coloured counties,
    And hear the larks so high
    About us in the sky.

---

[2] Pronounced Breedon.

The bells would ring to call her
    In valleys miles away:
"Come all to church, good people;
    Good people, come and pray."
But here my love would stay.

And I would turn and answer
    Among the springing thyme,
"Oh, peal upon our wedding,
    And we will hear the chime,
    And come to church in time."

But when the snows at Christmas
    On Bredon top were strown,
My love rose up so early
    And stole out unbeknown
    And went to church alone.

They tolled the one bell only,
    Groom there was none to see,
The mourners followed after,
    And so to church went she,
    And would not wait for me.

The bells they sound on Bredon,
    And still the steeples hum.
"Come all to church, good people,"—
    Oh, noisy bells, be dumb;
    I hear you, I will come.

XXII

The street sounds to the soldiers' tread,
    And out we troop to see:
A single redcoat turns his head,
    He turns and looks at me.

My man, from sky to sky's so far,
    We never crossed before;
Such leagues apart the world's ends are,
    We're like to meet no more;

What thoughts at heart have you and I
We cannot stop to tell;
But dead or living, drunk or dry,
Soldier, I wish you well.

XXIII

The lads in their hundreds to Ludlow come in for the fair,
    There's men from the barn and the forge and the mill and the fold,
The lads for the girls and the lads for the liquor are there,
    And there with the rest are the lads that will never be old.

There's chaps from the town and the field and the till and the cart,
    And many to count are the stalwart, and many the brave,
And many the handsome of face and the handsome of heart,
    And few that will carry their looks or their truth to the grave.

I wish one could know them, I wish there were tokens to tell
    The fortunate fellows that now you can never discern;
And then one could talk with them friendly and wish them farewell
    And watch them depart on the way that they will not return.

But now you may stare as you like and there's nothing to scan;
    And brushing your elbow unguessed-at and not to be told
They carry back bright to the coiner the mintage of man,
    The lads that will die in their glory and never be old.

XXIV

Say, lad, have you things to do?
    Quick then, while your day's at prime.
Quick, and if 'tis work for two,
    Here am I, man: now's your time.

Send me now, and I shall go;
    Call me, I shall hear you call;
Use me ere they lay me low
    Where a man's no use at all;

Ere the wholesome flesh decay,
    And the willing nerve be numb,
And the lips lack breath to say,
    "No, my lad, I cannot come."

XXV

This time of year a twelvemonth past,
    When Fred and I would meet,
We needs must jangle, till at last
    We fought and I was beat.

So then the summer fields about,
    Till rainy days began,
Rose Harland on her Sundays out
    Walked with the better man.

The better man she walks with still,
    Though now 'tis not with Fred:
A lad that lives and has his will
    Is worth a dozen dead.

Fred keeps the house all kinds of weather,
    And clay's the house he keeps;
When Rose and I walk out together
    Stock-still lies Fred and sleeps.

XXVI

    Along the fields as we came by
A year ago, my love and I,
The aspen over stile and stone
Was talking to itself alone.
"Oh who are these that kiss and pass?
A country lover and his lass;
Two lovers looking to be wed;
And time shall put them both to bed,
But she shall lie with earth above,
And he beside another love."

    And sure enough beneath the tree
There walks another love with me,
And overhead the aspen heaves
Its rainy-sounding silver leaves;
And I spell nothing in their stir,
But now perhaps they speak to her,
And plain for her to understand
They talk about a time at hand
When I shall sleep with clover clad,

And she beside another lad.

XXVII

"Is my team ploughing,
    That I was used to drive
And hear the harness jingle
    When I was man alive?"

Ay, the horses trample,
    The harness jingles now;
No change though you lie under
    The land you used to plough.

"Is football playing
    Along the river shore,
With lads to chase the leather,
    Now I stand up no more?"

Ay, the ball is flying,
    The lads play heart and soul;
The goal stands up, the keeper
    Stands up to keep the goal.

"Is my girl happy,
    That I thought hard to leave,
And has she tired of weeping
    As she lies down at eve?"

Ay, she lies down lightly,
    She lies not down to weep:
Your girl is well contented.
    Be still, my lad, and sleep.

"Is my friend hearty,
    Now I am thin and pine,
And has he found to sleep in
    A better bed than mine?"

Yes, lad, I lie easy,
    I lie as lads would choose;
I cheer a dead man's sweetheart,
    Never ask me whose.

XXVIII

THE WELSH MARCHES

High the vanes of Shrewsbury gleam
Islanded in Severn stream;
The bridges from the steepled crest
Cross the water east and west.

The flag of morn in conqueror's state
Enters at the English gate:
The vanquished eve, as night prevails,
Bleeds upon the road to Wales.

Ages since the vanquished bled
Round my mother's marriage-bed;
There the ravens feasted far
About the open house of war:

When Severn down to Buildwas ran
Coloured with the death of man,
Couched upon her brother's grave
The Saxon got me on the slave.

The sound of fight is silent long
That began the ancient wrong;
Long the voice of tears is still
That wept of old the endless ill.

In my heart it has not died,
The war that sleeps on Severn side;
They cease not fighting, east and west,
On the marches of my breast.

Here the truceless armies yet
Trample, rolled in blood and sweat;
They kill and kill and never die;
And I think that each is I.

None will part us, none undo
The knot that makes one flesh of two,
Sick with hatred, sick with pain,
Strangling—When shall we be slain?

When shall I be dead and rid
Of the wrong my father did?
How long, how long, till spade and hearse
Put to sleep my mother's curse?

XXIX

THE LENT LILY

'Tis spring; come out to ramble
    The hilly brakes around,
For under thorn and bramble
    About the hollow ground
    The primroses are found.

And there's the windflower chilly
    With all the winds at play,
And there's the Lenten lily
    That has not long to stay
    And dies on Easter day.

And since till girls go maying
    You find the primrose still,
And find the windflower playing
    With every wind at will,
    But not the daffodil,

Bring baskets now, and sally
    Upon the spring's array,
And bear from hill and valley
    The daffodil away
    That dies on Easter day.

XXX

Others, I am not the first,
Have willed more mischief than they durst:
If in the breathless night I too
Shiver now, 'tis nothing new.

More than I, if truth were told,
Have stood and sweated hot and cold,
And through their reins in ice and fire
Fear contended with desire.

Agued once like me were they,
But I like them shall win my way
Lastly to the bed of mould
Where there's neither heat nor cold.

But from my grave across my brow
Plays no wind of healing now,
And fire and ice within me fight
Beneath the suffocating night.

XXXI

On Wenlock Edge the wood's in trouble;
    His forest fleece the Wrekin heaves;
The gale, it plies the saplings double,
    And thick on Severn snow the leaves.

'Twould blow like this through holt and hanger
    When Uricon the city stood:
'Tis the old wind in the old anger,
    But then it threshed another wood.

Then, 'twas before my time, the Roman
    At yonder heaving hill would stare:
The blood that warms an English yeoman,
    The thoughts that hurt him, they were there.

There, like the wind through woods in riot,
    Through him the gale of life blew high;
The tree of man was never quiet:
    Then 'twas the Roman, now 'tis I.

The gale, it plies the saplings double,
    It blows so hard, 'twill soon be gone:
To-day the Roman and his trouble
    Are ashes under Uricon.

XXXII

From far, from eve and morning
    And yon twelve-winded sky,
The stuff of life to knit me
    Blew hither: here am I.

Now- for a breath I tarry
    Nor yet disperse apart—
Take my hand quick and tell me,
    What have you in your heart.

Speak now, and I will answer;
    How shall I help you, say;
Ere to the wind's twelve quarters
    I take my endless way.

XXXIII

If truth in hearts that perish
    Could move the powers on high,
I think the love I bear you
    Should make you not to die.

Sure, sure, if stedfast meaning,
    If single thought could save,
The world might end to-morrow,
    You should not see the grave.

This long and sure-set liking,
    This boundless will to please,
—Oh, you should live for ever
    If there were help in these.

But now, since all is idle,
    To this lost heart be kind,
Ere to a town you journey
    Where friends are ill to find.

XXXIV

THE NEW MISTRESS

"Oh, sick I am to see you, will you never let me be?
You may be good for something, but you are not good for me.
Oh, go where you are wanted, for you are not wanted here."
And that was all the farewell when I parted from my dear.

"I will go where I am wanted, to a lady born and bred
Who will dress me free for nothing in a uniform of red;
She will not be sick to see me if I only keep it clean:
I will go where I am wanted for a soldier of the Queen."

"I will go where I am wanted, for the sergeant does not mind;
He may be sick to see me but he treats me very kind:
He gives me beer and breakfast and a ribbon for my cap,
And I never knew a sweetheart spend her money on a chap."

"I will go where I am wanted, where there's room for one or two,
And the men are none too many for the work there is to do;
Where the standing line wears thinner and the dropping dead lie thick;
And the enemies of England they shall see me and be sick."

XXXV

On the idle hill of summer,
    Sleepy with the flow of streams,
Far I hear the steady drummer
    Drumming like a noise in dreams.

Far and near and low and louder
    On the roads of earth go by,
Dear to friends and food for powder,
    Soldiers marching, all to die.

East and west on fields forgotten
    Bleach the bones of comrades slain,
Lovely lads and dead and rotten;
    None that go return again.

Far the calling bugles hollo,
    High the screaming fife replies,
Gay the files of scarlet follow:
    Woman bore me, I will rise.

XXXVI

White in the moon the long road lies,
    The moon stands blank above;
White in the moon the long road lies
    That leads me from my love.

Still hangs the hedge without a gust,
    Still, still the shadows stay:
My feet upon the moonlit dust
    Pursue the ceaseless way.

The world is round, so travellers tell,
    And straight though reach the track,
Trudge on, trudge on, 'twill all be well,
    The way will guide one back.

But ere the circle homeward hies
    Far, far must it remove:
White in the moon the long road lies
    That leads me from my love.

XXXVII

    As through the wild green hills of Wyre
The train ran, changing sky and shire,
And far behind, a fading crest,
Low in the forsaken west
Sank the high-reared head of Clee,
My hand lay empty on my knee.
Aching on my knee it lay:
That morning half a shire away
So many an honest fellow's fist
Had well-nigh wrung it from the wrist.
Hand, said I, since now we part
From fields and men we know by heart,
From strangers' faces, strangers' lands,—
Hand, you have held true fellows' hands.
Be clean then; rot before you do
A thing they'd not believe of you.
You and I must keep from shame
In London streets the Shropshire name;
On banks of Thames they must not say
Severn breeds worse men than they;
And friends abroad must bear in mind
Friends at home they leave behind.
Oh, I shall be stiff and cold
When I forget you, hearts of gold;
The land where I shall mind you not
Is the land where all's forgot.
And if my foot returns no more

To Teme nor Corve nor Severn shore,
Luck, my lads, be with you still
By falling stream and standing hill,
By chiming tower and whispering tree,
Men that made a man of me.
About your work in town and farm
Still you'll keep my head from harm,
Still you'll help me, hands that gave
A grasp to friend me to the grave.

XXXVIII

The winds out of the west land blow,
    My friends have breathed them there;
Warm with the blood of lads I know
    Comes east the sighing air.

It fanned their temples, filled their lungs,
    Scattered their forelocks free;
My friends made words of it with tongues
    That talk no more to me.

Their voices, dying as they fly,
    Thick on the wind are sown;
The names of men blow soundless by,
    My fellows' and my own.

Oh lads, at home I heard you plain,
    But here your speech is still,
And down the sighing wind in vain
    You hollo from the hill.

The wind and I, we both were there,
    But neither long abode;
Now through the friendless world we fare
    And sigh upon the road.

XXXIX

'Tis time, I think by Wenlock town
    The golden broom should blow;
The hawthorn sprinkled up and down
    Should charge the land with snow.

Spring will not wait the loiterer's time
    Who keeps so long away;
So others wear the broom and climb
    The hedgerows heaped with may.

Oh tarnish late on Wenlock Edge,
    Gold that I never see;
Lie long, high snowdrifts in the hedge
    That will not shower on me.

XL

Into my heart an air that kills
    From yon far country blows:
What are those blue remembered hills,
    What spires, what farms are those?

That is the land of lost content,
    I see it shining plain,
The happy highways where I went
    And cannot come again.

XLI

    In my own shire, if I was sad
Homely comforters I had:
The earth, because my heart was sore,
Sorrowed for the son she bore;
And standing hills, long to remain,
Shared their short-lived comrade's pain.
And bound for the same bourn as I,
On every road I wandered by,
Trod beside me, close and dear,
The beautiful and death-struck year:
Whether in the woodland brown
I heard the beechnut rustle down,
And saw the purple crocus pale
Flower about the autumn dale;
Or littering far the fields of May
Lady-smocks a-bleaching lay,
And like a skylit water stood
The bluebells in the azured wood.

Yonder, lightening other loads,
The seasons range the country roads,
But here in London streets I ken
No such helpmates, only men;
And these are not in plight to bear,
If they would, another's care.
They have enough as 'tis: I see
In many an eye that measures me
The mortal sickness of a mind
Too unhappy to be kind.
Undone with misery, all they can
Is to hate their fellow man;
And till they drop they needs must still
Look at you and wish you ill.

XLII

THE MERRY GUIDE

Once in the wind of morning
    I ranged the thymy wold;
The world-wide air was azure
    And all the brooks ran gold.

There through the dews beside me
    Behold a youth that trod,
With feathered cap on forehead,
    And poised a golden rod.

With mien to match the morning
    And gay delightful guise
And friendly brows and laughter
    He looked me in the eyes.

Oh whence, I asked, and whither?
    He smiled and would not say,
And looked at me and beckoned
    And laughed and led the way.

And with kind looks and laughter
    And nought to say beside
We two went on together,
    I and my happy guide.

Across the glittering pastures
    And empty upland still
And solitude of shepherds
    High in the folded hill,

By hanging woods and hamlets
    That gaze through orchards down
On many a windmill turning
    And far-discovered town,

With gay regards of promise
    And sure unslackened stride
And smiles and nothing spoken
    Led on my merry guide.

By blowing realms of woodland
    With sunstruck vanes afield
And cloud-led shadows sailing
    About the windy weald,

By valley-guarded granges
    And silver waters wide,
Content at heart I followed
    With my delightful guide.

And like the cloudy shadows
    Across the country blown
We two face on for ever,
    But not we two alone.

With the great gale we journey
    That breathes from gardens thinned,
Borne in the drift of blossoms
    Whose petals throng the wind;

Buoyed on the heaven-heard whisper
    Of dancing leaflets whirled
From all the woods that autumn
    Bereaves in all the world.

And midst the fluttering legion
    Of all that ever died
I follow, and before us
    Goes the delightful guide,

With lips that brim with laughter
  But never once respond,
And feet that fly on feathers,
  And serpent-circled wand.

XLIII

THE IMMORTAL PART

When I meet the morning beam,
Or lay me down at night to dream,
I hear my bones within me say,
"Another night, another day."

"When shall this slough of sense be cast,
This dust of thoughts be laid at last,
The man of flesh and soul be slain
And the man of bone remain?"

"This tongue that talks, these lungs that shout,
These thews that hustle us about,
This brain that fills the skull with schemes,
And its humming hive of dreams,-"

"These to-day are proud in power
And lord it in their little hour:
The immortal bones obey control
Of dying flesh and dying soul."

"'Tis long till eve and morn are gone:
Slow the endless night comes on,
And late to fulness grows the birth
That shall last as long as earth."

"Wanderers eastward, wanderers west,
Know you why you cannot rest?
'Tis that every mother's son
Travails with a skeleton."

"Lie down in the bed of dust;
Bear the fruit that bear you must;
Bring the eternal seed to light,
And morn is all the same as night."

"Rest you so from trouble sore,
Fear the heat o' the sun no more,
Nor the snowing winter wild,
Now you labour not with child."

"Empty vessel, garment cast,
We that wore you long shall last.
—Another night, another day."
So my bones within me say.

Therefore they shall do my will
To-day while I am master still,
And flesh and soul, now both are strong,
Shall hale the sullen slaves along,

Before this fire of sense decay,
This smoke of thought blow clean away,
And leave with ancient night alone
The stedfast and enduring bone.

XLIV

Shot? so quick, so clean an ending?
    Oh that was right, lad, that was brave:
Yours was not an ill for mending,
    'Twas best to take it to the grave.

Oh you had forethought, you could reason,
    And saw your road and where it led,
And early wise and brave in season
    Put the pistol to your head.

Oh soon, and better so than later
    After long disgrace and scorn,
You shot dead the household traitor,
    The soul that should not have been born.

Right you guessed the rising morrow
    And scorned to tread the mire you must:
Dust's your wages, son of sorrow,
    But men may come to worse than dust.

Souls undone, undoing others,—
    Long time since the tale began.
You would not live to wrong your brothers:
    Oh lad, you died as fits a man.

Now to your grave shall friend and stranger
    With ruth and some with envy come:
Undishonoured, clear of danger,
    Clean of guilt, pass hence and home.

Turn safe to rest, no dreams, no waking;
    And here, man, here's the wreath I've made:
'Tis not a gift that's worth the taking,
    But wear it and it will not fade.

XLV

If it chance your eye offend you,
    Pluck it out, lad, and be sound:
'Twill hurt, but here are salves to friend you,
    And many a balsam grows on ground.

And if your hand or foot offend you,
    Cut it off, lad, and be whole;
But play the man, stand up and end you,
    When your sickness is your soul.

XLVI

    Bring, in this timeless grave to throw,
No cypress, sombre on the snow;
Snap not from the bitter yew
His leaves that live December through;
Break no rosemary, bright with rime
And sparkling to the cruel clime;
Nor plod the winter land to look
For willows in the icy brook
To cast them leafless round him: bring
No spray that ever buds in spring.

    But if the Christmas field has kept
Awns the last gleaner overstept,
Or shrivelled flax, whose flower is blue
A single season, never two;

Or if one haulm whose year is o'er
Shivers on the upland frore,
—Oh, bring from hill and stream and plain
Whatever will not flower again,
To give him comfort: he and those
Shall bide eternal bedfellows
Where low upon the couch he lies
Whence he never shall arise.

XLVII

THE CARPENTER'S SON

"Here the hangman stops his cart:
Now the best of friends must part.
Fare you well, for ill fare I:
Live, lads, and I will die."

"Oh, at home had I but stayed
'Prenticed to my father's trade,
Had I stuck to plane and adze,
I had not been lost, my lads."

"Then I might have built perhaps
Gallows-trees for other chaps,
Never dangled on my own,
Had I but left ill alone."

"Now, you see, they hang me high,
And the people passing by
Stop to shake their fists and curse;
So 'tis come from ill to worse."

"Here hang I, and right and left
Two poor fellows hang for theft:
All the same's the luck we prove,
Though the midmost hangs for love."

"Comrades all, that stand and gaze,
Walk henceforth in other ways;
See my neck and save your own:
Comrades all, leave ill alone."

"Make some day a decent end,
Shrewder fellows than your friend.
Fare you well, for ill fare I:
Live, lads, and I will die."

XLVIII

Be still, my soul, be still; the arms you bear are brittle,
    Earth and high heaven are fixt of old and founded strong.
Think rather,—call to thought, if now you grieve a little,
    The days when we had rest, O soul, for they were long.

Men loved unkindness then, but lightless in the quarry
    I slept and saw not; tears fell down, I did not mourn;
Sweat ran and blood sprang out and I was never sorry:
    Then it was well with me, in days ere I was born.

Now, and I muse for why and never find the reason,
    I pace the earth, and drink the air, and feel the sun.
Be still, be still, my soul; it is but for a season:
    Let us endure an hour and see injustice done.

Ay, look: high heaven and earth ail from the prime foundation;
    All thoughts to rive the heart are here, and all are vain:
Horror and scorn and hate and fear and indignation—
    Oh why did I awake? when shall I sleep again?

XLIX

Think no more, lad; laugh, be jolly:
    Why should men make haste to die?
Empty heads and tongues a-talking
Make the rough road easy walking,
And the feather pate of folly
    Bears the falling sky.

Oh, 'tis jesting, dancing, drinking
    Spins the heavy world around.
If young hearts were not so clever,
Oh, they would be young for ever:
Think no more; 'tis only thinking
    Lays lads underground.

L

Clunton and Clunbury,
    Clungunford and Clun,
Are the quietest places
    Under the sun.

In valleys of springs of rivers,
    By Ony and Teme and Clun,
The country for easy livers,
    The quietest under the sun,

We still had sorrows to lighten,
    One could not be always glad,
And lads knew trouble at Knighton
    When I was a Knighton lad.

By bridges that Thames runs under,
    In London, the town built ill,
'Tis sure small matter for wonder
    If sorrow is with one still.

And if as a lad grows older
    The troubles he bears are more,
He carries his griefs on a shoulder
    That handselled them long before.

Where shall one halt to deliver
    This luggage I'd lief set down?
Not Thames, not Teme is the river,
    Nor London nor Knighton the town:

'Tis a long way further than Knighton,
    A quieter place than Clun,
Where doomsday may thunder and lighten
    And little 'twill matter to one.

LI

    Loitering with a vacant eye
Along the Grecian gallery,
And brooding on my heavy ill,
I met a statue standing still.
Still in marble stone stood he,

And stedfastly he looked at me.
"Well met," I thought the look would say,
"We both were fashioned far away;
We neither knew, when we were young,
These Londoners we live among."

    Still he stood and eyed me hard,
An earnest and a grave regard:
"What, lad, drooping with your lot?
I too would be where I am not.
I too survey that endless line
Of men whose thoughts are not as mine.
Years, ere you stood up from rest,
On my neck the collar prest;
Years, when you lay down your ill,
I shall stand and bear it still.
Courage, lad, 'tis not for long:
Stand, quit you like stone, be strong."
So I thought his look would say;
And light on me my trouble lay,
And I slept out in flesh and bone
Manful like the man of stone.

LII

Far in a western brookland
    That bred me long ago
The poplars stand and tremble
    By pools I used to know.

There, in the windless night-time,
    The wanderer, marvelling why,
Halts on the bridge to hearken
    How soft the poplars sigh.

He hears: long since forgotten
    In fields where I was known,
Here I lie down in London
    And turn to rest alone.

There, by the starlit fences,
    The wanderer halts and hears
My soul that lingers sighing
    About the glimmering weirs.

LIII

THE TRUE LOVER

The lad came to the door at night,
    When lovers crown their vows,
And whistled soft and out of sight
    In shadow of the boughs.

"I shall not vex you with my face
    Henceforth, my love, for aye;
So take me in your arms a space
    Before the east is grey."

"When I from hence away am past
    I shall not find a bride,
And you shall be the first and last
    I ever lay beside."

She heard and went and knew not why;
    Her heart to his she laid;
Light was the air beneath the sky
    But dark under the shade.

"Oh do you breathe, lad, that your breast
    Seems not to rise and fall,
And here upon my bosom prest
    There beats no heart at all?"

"Oh loud, my girl, it once would knock,
    You should have felt it then;
But since for you I stopped the clock
    It never goes again."

"Oh lad, what is it, lad, that drips
    Wet from your neck on mine?
What is it falling on my lips,
    My lad, that tastes of brine?"

"Oh like enough 'tis blood, my dear,
    For when the knife has slit
The throat across from ear to ear
    'Twill bleed because of it."

Under the stars the air was light
    But dark below the boughs,
The still air of the speechless night,
    When lovers crown their vows.

LIV

With rue my heart is laden
    For golden friends I had,
For many a rose-lipt maiden
    And many a lightfoot lad.

By brooks too broad for leaping
    The lightfoot boys are laid;
The rose-lipt girls are sleeping
    In fields where roses fade.

LV

Westward on the high-hilled plains
    Where for me the world began,
Still, I think, in newer veins
    Frets the changeless blood of man.

Now that other lads than I
    Strip to bathe on Severn shore,
They, no help, for all they try,
    Tread the mill I trod before.

There, when hueless is the west
    And the darkness hushes wide,
Where the lad lies down to rest
    Stands the troubled dream beside.

There, on thoughts that once were mine,
    Day looks down the eastern steep,
And the youth at morning shine
    Makes the vow he will not keep.

LVI

THE DAY OF BATTLE

"Far I hear the bugle blow
To call me where I would not go,
And the guns begin the song,
'Soldier, fly or stay for long.'"

"Comrade, if to turn and fly
Made a soldier never die,
Fly I would, for who would not?
'Tis sure no pleasure to be shot."

"But since the man that runs away
Lives to die another day,
And cowards' funerals, when they come
Are not wept so well at home."

"Therefore, though the best is bad,
Stand and do the best my lad;
Stand and fight and see your slain,
And take the bullet in your brain."

LVII

You smile upon your friend to-day,
    To-day his ills are over;
You hearken to the lover's say,
    And happy is the lover.

'Tis late to hearken, late to smile,
    But better late than never:
I shall have lived a little while
    Before I die for ever.

LVIII

When I came last to Ludlow
    Amidst the moonlight pale,
Two friends kept step beside me,
    Two honest lads and hale.

Now Dick lies long in the churchyard,
    And Ned lies long in jail,
And I come home to Ludlow
    Amidst the moonlight pale.

LIX

THE ISLE OF PORTLAND

The star-filled seas are smooth to-night
    From France to England strown;
Black towers above the Portland light
    The felon-quarried stone.

On yonder island, not to rise,
    Never to stir forth free,
Far from his folk a dead lad lies
    That once was friends with me.

Lie you easy, dream you light,
    And sleep you fast for aye;
And luckier may you find the night
    Than ever you found the day.

LX

Now hollow fires burn out to black,
    And lights are guttering low:
Square your shoulders, lift your pack,
    And leave your friends and go.

Oh never fear, man, nought's to dread,
    Look not left nor right:
In all the endless road you tread
    There's nothing but the night.

LXI

HUGHLEY STEEPLE

The vane on Hughley steeple
Veers bright, a far-known sign,
And there lie Hughley people,
And there lie friends of mine.

Tall in their midst the tower
Divides the shade and sun,
And the clock strikes the hour
And tells the time to none.

To south the headstones cluster,
The sunny mounds lie thick;
The dead are more in muster
At Hughley than the quick.
North, for a soon-told number,
Chill graves the sexton delves,
And steeple-shadowed slumber
The slayers of themselves.

To north, to south, lie parted,
With Hughley tower above,
The kind, the single-hearted,
The lads I used to love.
And, south or north, 'tis only
A choice of friends one knows,
And I shall ne'er be lonely
Asleep with these or those.

LXII

"Terence, this is stupid stuff:
You eat your victuals fast enough;
There can't be much amiss, 'tis clear,
To see the rate you drink your beer.
But oh, good Lord, the verse you make,
It gives a chap the belly-ache.
The cow, the old cow, she is dead;
It sleeps well, the horned head:
We poor lads, 'tis our turn now
To hear such tunes as killed the cow.
Pretty friendship 'tis to rhyme
Your friends to death before their time
Moping melancholy mad:
Come, pipe a tune to dance to, lad."

Why, if 'tis dancing you would be,
There's brisker pipes than poetry.
Say, for what were hop-yards meant,
Or why was Burton built on Trent?
Oh many a peer of England brews

Livelier liquor than the Muse,
And malt does more than Milton can
To justify God's ways to man.
Ale, man, ale's the stuff to drink
For fellows whom it hurts to think:
Look into the pewter pot
To see the world as the world's not.
And faith, 'tis pleasant till 'tis past:
The mischief is that 'twill not last.
Oh I have been to Ludlow fair
And left my necktie God knows where,
And carried half-way home, or near,
Pints and quarts of Ludlow beer:
Then the world seemed none so bad,
And I myself a sterling lad;
And down in lovely muck I've lain,
Happy till I woke again.
Then I saw the morning sky:
Heigho, the tale was all a lie;
The world, it was the old world yet,
I was I, my things were wet,
And nothing now remained to do
But begin the game anew.

Therefore, since the world has still
Much good, but much less good than ill,
And while the sun and moon endure
Luck's a chance, but trouble's sure,
I'd face it as a wise man would,
And train for ill and not for good.
'Tis true the stuff I bring for sale
Is not so brisk a brew as ale:
Out of a stem that scored the hand
I wrung it in a weary land.
But take it: if the smack is sour,
The better for the embittered hour;
It should do good to heart and head
When your soul is in my soul's stead;
And I will friend you, if I may,
In the dark and cloudy day.

There was a king reigned in the East:
There, when kings will sit to feast,
They get their fill before they think
With poisoned meat and poisoned drink.

He gathered all that springs to birth
From the many-venomed earth;
First a little, thence to more,
He sampled all her killing store;
And easy, smiling, seasoned sound,
Sate the king when healths went round.
They put arsenic in his meat
And stared aghast to watch him eat;
They poured strychnine in his cup
And shook to see him drink it up:
They shook, they stared as white's their shirt:
Them it was their poison hurt.
—I tell the tale that I heard told.
Mithridates, he died old.

LXIII

I hoed and trenched and weeded,
    And took the flowers to fair:
I brought them home unheeded;
    The hue was not the wear.

So up and down I sow them
    For lads like me to find,
When I shall lie below them,
    A dead man out of mind.

Some seed the birds devour,
    And some the season mars,
But here and there will flower
    The solitary stars,

And fields will yearly bear them
    As light-leaved spring comes on,
And luckless lads will wear them
    When I am dead and gone.

LAST POEMS

I publish these poems, few though they are, because it is not likely that I shall ever be impelled to write much more. I can no longer expect to be revisited by the continuous excitement under which in the early months of 1895 I wrote the greater part of my first book, nor indeed could I well sustain it if it came; and it is best that what I have written should be printed while I am here to see it through the press and control its spelling and punctuation. About a quarter of this matter belongs to the April of the present year, but most of it to dates between 1895 and 1910.

September 1922

We'll to the woods no more,
The laurels are all cut,
The bowers are bare of bay
That once the Muses wore;
The year draws in the day
And soon will evening shut:
The laurels all are cut,
We'll to the woods no more.
Oh we'll no more, no more
To the leafy woods away,
To the high wild woods of laurel
And the bowers of bay no more.

I.

THE WEST

Beyond the moor and the mountain crest
—Comrade, look not on the west—
The sun is down and drinks away
From air and land the lees of day.

The long cloud and the single pine
Sentinel the ending line,
And out beyond it, clear and wan,
Reach the gulfs of evening on.

The son of woman turns his brow
West from forty countries now,
And, as the edge of heaven he eyes,
Thinks eternal thoughts, and sighs.

Oh wide's the world, to rest or roam,
With change abroad and cheer at home,
Fights and furloughs, talk and tale,
Company and beef and ale.

But if I front the evening sky
Silent on the west look I,
And my comrade, stride for stride,
Paces silent at my side,

Comrade, look not on the west:
'Twill have the heart out of your breast;
'Twill take your thoughts and sink them far,
Leagues beyond the sunset bar.

Oh lad, I fear that yon's the sea
Where they fished for you and me,
And there, from whence we both were ta'en,
You and I shall drown again.

Send not on your soul before
To dive from that beguiling shore,
And let not yet the swimmer leave
His clothes upon the sands of eve.

Too fast to yonder strand forlorn
We journey, to the sunken bourn,
To flush the fading tinges eyed
By other lads at eventide.

Wide is the world, to rest or roam,
And early 'tis for turning home:
Plant your heel on earth and stand,
And let's forget our native land.

When you and I are split on air
Long we shall be strangers there;
Friends of flesh and bone are best;
Comrade, look not on the west.

II.

As I gird on for fighting
    My sword upon my thigh,
I think on old ill fortunes
    Of better men than I.

Think I, the round world over,
    What golden lads are low
With hurts not mine to mourn for
    And shames I shall not know.

What evil luck soever
    For me remains in store,
'Tis sure much finer fellows
    Have fared much worse before.

So here are things to think on
    That ought to make me brave,
As I strap on for fighting
    My sword that will not save.

III.

Her strong enchantments failing,
    Her towers of fear in wreck,
Her limbecks dried of poisons
    And the knife at her neck,

The Queen of air and darkness
    Begins to shrill and cry,
'O young man, O my slayer,
    To-morrow you shall die.'

O Queen of air and darkness,
    I think 'tis truth you say,
And I shall die to-morrow;
    But you will die to-day.

IV.

ILLIC JACET

Oh hard is the bed they have made him,
    And common the blanket and cheap;
But there he will lie as they laid him:
    Where else could you trust him to sleep?

To sleep when the bugle is crying
    And cravens have heard and are brave,
When mothers and sweethearts are sighing
    And lads are in love with the grave.

Oh dark is the chamber and lonely,
    And lights and companions depart;
But lief will he lose them and only
    Behold the desire of his heart.

And low is the roof, but it covers
    A sleeper content to repose;
And far from his friends and his lovers
    He lies with the sweetheart he chose.

V.

GRENADIER

The Queen she sent to look for me,
    The sergeant he did say,
'Young man, a soldier will you be
    For thirteen pence a day?'

For thirteen pence a day did I
    Take off the things I wore,
And I have marched to where I lie,
    And I shall march no more.

My mouth is dry, my shirt is wet,
    My blood runs all away,
So now I shall not die in debt
    For thirteen pence a day.

To-morrow after new young men
    The sergeant he must see,
For things will all be over then
    Between the Queen and me.

And I shall have to bate my price,
    For in the grave, they say,
Is neither knowledge nor device
    Nor thirteen pence a day.

VI.

LANCER

I 'listed at home for a lancer,
    Oh who would not sleep with the brave?
I 'listed at home for a lancer
    To ride on a horse to my grave.

And over the seas we were bidden
    A country to take and to keep;
And far with the brave I have ridden,
    And now with the brave I shall sleep.

For round me the men will be lying
    That learned me the way to behave.
And showed me my business of dying:
    Oh who would not sleep with the brave?

They ask and there is not an answer;
Says I, I will 'list for a lancer,
    Oh who would not sleep with the brave?

And I with the brave shall be sleeping
    At ease on my mattress of loam,
When back from their taking and keeping
    The squadron is riding home.

The wind with the plumes will be playing,
    The girls will stand watching them wave,
And eyeing my comrades and saying
    Oh who would not sleep with the brave?

They ask and there is not an answer;
Says you, I will 'list for a lancer,
Oh who would not sleep with the brave?

VII.

In valleys green and still
    Where lovers wander maying
They hear from over hill
    A music playing.

Behind the drum and fife,
    Past hawthornwood and hollow,
Through earth and out of life
    The soldiers follow.

The soldier's is the trade:
    In any wind or weather
He steals the heart of maid
    And man together.

The lover and his lass
    Beneath the hawthorn lying
Have heard the soldiers pass,
    And both are sighing.

And down the distance they
    With dying note and swelling
Walk the resounding way
    To the still dwelling.

VIII.

Soldier from the wars returning,
    Spoiler of the taken town,
Here is ease that asks not earning;
    Turn you in and sit you down.

Peace is come and wars are over,
    Welcome you and welcome all,
While the charger crops the clover
    And his bridle hangs in stall.

Now no more of winters biting,
    Filth in trench from fall to spring,
Summers full of sweat and fighting
    For the Kesar or the King.

Rest you, charger, rust you, bridle;
    Kings and kesars, keep your pay;
Soldier, sit you down and idle
    At the inn of night for aye.

IX.

The chestnut casts his flambeaux, and the flowers
    Stream from the hawthorn on the wind away,
The doors clap to, the pane is blind with showers.
    Pass me the can, lad; there's an end of May.

There's one spoilt spring to scant our mortal lot,
    One season ruined of our little store.
May will be fine next year as like as not:
    Oh ay, but then we shall be twenty-four.

We for a certainty are not the first
    Have sat in taverns while the tempest hurled
Their hopeful plans to emptiness, and cursed
    Whatever brute and blackguard made the world.

It is in truth iniquity on high
    To cheat our sentenced souls of aught they crave,
And mar the merriment as you and I
    Fare on our long fool's-errand to the grave.

Iniquity it is; but pass the can.
    My lad, no pair of kings our mothers bore;
Our only portion is the estate of man:
    We want the moon, but we shall get no more.

If here to-day the cloud of thunder lours
    To-morrow it will hie on far behests;
The flesh will grieve on other bones than ours
    Soon, and the soul will mourn in other breasts.

The troubles of our proud and angry dust
    Are from eternity, and shall not fail.
Bear them we can, and if we can we must.
    Shoulder the sky, my lad, and drink your ale.

X.

Could man be drunk for ever
    With liquor, love, or fights,
Lief should I rouse at morning
    And lief lie down of nights.

But men at whiles are sober
    And think by fits and starts,
And if they think, they fasten
    Their hands upon their hearts.

XI.

Yonder see the morning blink:
    The sun is up, and up must I,
To wash and dress and eat and drink
And look at things and talk and think
    And work, and God knows why.

Oh often have I washed and dressed
    And what's to show for all my pain?
Let me lie abed and rest:
Ten thousand times I've done my best
    And all's to do again.

XII.

    The laws of God, the laws of man,
He may keep that will and can;
Now I: let God and man decree
Laws for themselves and not for me;
And if my ways are not as theirs
Let them mind their own affairs.
Their deeds I judge and much condemn,
Yet when did I make laws for them?
Please yourselves, say I, and they
Need only look the other way.
But no, they will not; they must still

Wrest their neighbour to their will,
And make me dance as they desire
With jail and gallows and hell-fire.
And how am I to face the odds
Of man's bedevilment and God's?
I, a stranger and afraid
In a world I never made.
They will be master, right or wrong;
Though both are foolish, both are strong,
And since, my soul, we cannot fly
To Saturn or Mercury,
Keep we must, if keep we can,
These foreign laws of God and man.

XIII.

THE DESERTER

"What sound awakened me, I wonder,
    For now 'tis dumb."
"Wheels on the road most like, or thunder:
    Lie down; 'twas not the drum.:

"Toil at sea and two in haven
    And trouble far:
Fly, crow, away, and follow, raven,
    And all that croaks for war."

"Hark, I heard the bugle crying,
    And where am I?
My friends are up and dressed and dying,
    And I will dress and die."

"Oh love is rare and trouble plenty
    And carrion cheap,
And daylight dear at four-and-twenty:
    Lie down again and sleep."

"Reach me my belt and leave your prattle:
    Your hour is gone;
But my day is the day of battle,
    And that comes dawning on.

"They mow the field of man in season:
    Farewell, my fair,
And, call it truth or call it treason,
    Farewell the vows that were."

"Ay, false heart, forsake me lightly:
    'Tis like the brave.
They find no bed to joy in rightly
    Before they find the grave.

"Their love is for their own undoing.
    And east and west
They scour about the world a-wooing
    The bullet in their breast.

"Sail away the ocean over,
    Oh sail away,
And lie there with your leaden lover
    For ever and a day."

XIV.

THE CULPRIT

The night my father got me
    His mind was not on me;
He did not plague his fancy
    To muse if I should be
    The son you see.

The day my mother bore me
    She was a fool and glad,
For all the pain I cost her,
    That she had borne the lad
    That borne she had.

My mother and my father
    Out of the light they lie;
The warrant would not find them,
    And here 'tis only I
    Shall hang so high.

Oh let not man remember
    The soul that God forgot,
But fetch the county kerchief
    And noose me in the knot,
    And I will rot.

For so the game is ended
    That should not have begun.
My father and my mother
    They had a likely son,
    And I have none.

XV.

EIGHT O'CLOCK

He stood, and heard the steeple
    Sprinkle the quarters on the morning town.
One, two, three, four, to market-place and people
    It tossed them down.

Strapped, noosed, nighing his hour,
    He stood and counted them and cursed his luck;
And then the clock collected in the tower
    Its strength, and struck.

XVI.

SPRING MORNING

Star and coronal and bell
    April underfoot renews,
And the hope of man as well
    Flowers among the morning dews.

Now the old come out to look,
    Winter past and winter's pains.
How the sky in pool and brook
    Glitters on the grassy plains.

Easily the gentle air
    Wafts the turning season on;
Things to comfort them are there,
    Though 'tis true the best are gone.

Now the scorned unlucky lad
    Rousing from his pillow gnawn
Mans his heart and deep and glad
    Drinks the valiant air of dawn.

Half the night he longed to die,
    Now are sown on hill and plain
Pleasures worth his while to try
    Ere he longs to die again.

Blue the sky from east to west
    Arches, and the world is wide,
Though the girl he loves the best
    Rouses from another's side.

XVII.

ASTRONOMY

The Wain upon the northern steep
    Descends and lifts away.
Oh I will sit me down and weep
    For bones in Africa.

For pay and medals, name and rank,
    Things that he has not found,
He hove the Cross to heaven and sank
    The pole-star underground.

And now he does not even see
    Signs of the nadir roll
At night over the ground where he
    Is buried with the pole.

XVIII.

The rain, it streams on stone and hillock,
    The boot clings to the clay.
Since all is done that's due and right
Let's home; and now, my lad, good-night,
    For I must turn away.

Good-night, my lad, for nought's eternal;
    No league of ours, for sure.
Tomorrow I shall miss you less,
And ache of heart and heaviness
    Are things that time should cure.

Over the hill the highway marches
    And what's beyond is wide:
Oh soon enough will pine to nought
Remembrance and the faithful thought
    That sits the grave beside.

The skies, they are not always raining
    Nor grey the twelvemonth through;
And I shall meet good days and mirth,
And range the lovely lands of earth
    With friends no worse than you.

But oh, my man, the house is fallen
    That none can build again;
My man, how full of joy and woe
Your mother bore you years ago
    To-night to lie in the rain.

XIX.

In midnights of November,
    When Dead Man's Fair is nigh,
And danger in the valley,
    And anger in the sky,

Around the huddling homesteads
    The leafless timber roars,
And the dead call the dying
    And finger at the doors.

Oh, yonder faltering fingers
    Are hands I used to hold;
Their false companion drowses
    And leaves them in the cold.

Oh, to the bed of ocean,
    To Africk and to Ind,
I will arise and follow
    Along the rainy wind.

The night goes out and under
    With all its train forlorn;
Hues in the east assemble
    And cocks crow up the morn.

The living are the living
    And dead the dead will stay,
And I will sort with comrades
    That face the beam of day.

XX.

The night is freezing fast,
    To-morrow comes December;
        And winterfalls of old
Are with me from the past;
    And chiefly I remember
        How Dick would hate the cold.

Fall, winter, fall; for he,
    Prompt hand and headpiece clever,
        Has woven a winter robe,
And made of earth and sea
    His overcoat for ever,
        And wears the turning globe.

XXI.

The fairies break their dances
    And leave the printed lawn,
And up from India glances
    The silver sail of dawn.

The candles burn their sockets,
    The blinds let through the day,
The young man feels his pockets
    And wonders what's to pay.

XXII.

The sloe was lost in flower,
  The April elm was dim;
That was the lover's hour,
  The hour for lies and him.

If thorns are all the bower,
  If north winds freeze the fir,
Why, 'tis another's hour,
  The hour for truth and her.

XXIII.

In the morning, in the morning,
  In the happy field of hay,
Oh they looked at one another
  By the light of day.

In the blue and silver morning
  On the haycock as they lay,
Oh they looked at one another
  And they looked away.

XXIV.

EPITHALAMIUM

He is here, Urania's son,
Hymen come from Helicon;
God that glads the lover's heart,
He is here to join and part.
So the groomsman quits your side
And the bridegroom seeks the bride:
Friend and comrade yield you o'er
To her that hardly loves you more.

Now the sun his skyward beam
Has tilted from the Ocean stream.
Light the Indies, laggard sun:
Happy bridegroom, day is done,
And the star from OEta's steep
Calls to bed but not to sleep.

Happy bridegroom, Hesper brings
    All desired and timely things.
    All whom morning sends to roam,
    Hesper loves to lead them home.
    Home return who him behold,
    Child to mother, sheep to fold,
    Bird to nest from wandering wide:
    Happy bridegroom, seek your bride.

    Pour it out, the golden cup
    Given and guarded, brimming up,
    Safe through jostling markets borne
    And the thicket of the thorn;
    Folly spurned and danger past,
    Pour it to the god at last.

    Now, to smother noise and light,
    Is stolen abroad the wildering night,
    And the blotting shades confuse
    Path and meadow full of dews;
    And the high heavens, that all control,
    Turn in silence round the pole.
    Catch the starry beams they shed
    Prospering the marriage bed,
    And breed the land that reared your prime
    Sons to stay the rot of time.
    All is quiet, no alarms;
    Nothing fear of nightly harms.
    Safe you sleep on guarded ground,
    And in silent circle round
    The thoughts of friends keep watch and ward,
    Harnessed angels, hand on sword.

XXV.

THE ORACLES

'Tis mute, the word they went to hear on high Dodona mountain
    When winds were in the oakenshaws and all the cauldrons tolled,
And mute's the midland navel-stone beside the singing fountain,
    And echoes list to silence now where gods told lies of old.

I took my question to the shrine that has not ceased from speaking,
    The heart within, that tells the truth and tells it twice as plain;
And from the cave of oracles I heard the priestess shrieking
    That she and I should surely die and never live again.

Oh priestess, what you cry is clear, and sound good sense I think it;
    But let the screaming echoes rest, and froth your mouth no more.
'Tis true there's better boose than brine, but he that drowns must drink it;
    And oh, my lass, the news is news that men have heard before.

The King with half the East at heel is marched from lands of morning;
    Their fighters drink the rivers up, their shafts benight the air.
And he that stands will die for nought, and home there's no returning.
    The Spartans on the sea-wet rock sat down and combed their hair.

XXVI.

The half-moon westers low, my love,
    And the wind brings up the rain;
And wide apart lie we, my love,
    And seas between the twain.

I know not if it rains, my love,
    In the land where you do lie;
And oh, so sound you sleep, my love,
    You know no more than I.

XXVII.

The sigh that heaves the grasses
    Whence thou wilt never rise
Is of the air that passes
    And knows not if it sighs.

The diamond tears adorning
    Thy low mound on the lea,
Those are the tears of morning,
    That weeps, but not for thee.

XXVIII.

Now dreary dawns the eastern light,
    And fall of eve is drear,
And cold the poor man lies at night,
    And so goes out the year.

Little is the luck I've had,
    And oh, 'tis comfort small
To think that many another lad
    Has had no luck at all.

XXIX.

Wake not for the world-heard thunder
    Nor the chime that earthquakes toll.
Star may plot in heaven with planet,
Lightning rive the rock of granite,
Tempest tread the oakwood under:
    Fear not you for flesh nor soul.
Marching, fighting, victory past,
Stretch your limbs in peace at last.

Stir not for the soldiers drilling
    Nor the fever nothing cures:
Throb of drum and timbal's rattle
Call but man alive to battle,
And the fife with death-notes filling
    Screams for blood but not for yours.
Times enough you bled your best;
Sleep on now, and take your rest.

Sleep, my lad; the French are landed,
    London's burning, Windsor's down;
Clasp your cloak of earth about you,
We must man the ditch without you,
March unled and fight short-handed,
    Charge to fall and swim to drown.
Duty, friendship, bravery o'er,
Sleep away, lad; wake no more.

XXX.

SINNER'S RUE

I walked alone and thinking,
    And faint the nightwind blew
And stirred on mounds at crossways
    The flower of sinner's rue.

Where the roads part they bury
    Him that his own hand slays,
And so the weed of sorrow
    Springs at the four cross ways.

By night I plucked it hueless,
    When morning broke 'twas blue:
Blue at my breast I fastened
    The flower of sinner's rue.

It seemed a herb of healing,
    A balsam and a sign,
Flower of a heart whose trouble
    Must have been worse than mine.

Dead clay that did me kindness,
    I can do none to you,
But only wear for breastknot
    The flower of sinner's rue.

XXXI.

HELL'S GATE

    Onward led the road again
Through the sad uncoloured plain
Under twilight brooding dim,
And along the utmost rim
Wall and rampart risen to sight
Cast a shadow not of night,
And beyond them seemed to glow
Bonfires lighted long ago.
And my dark conductor broke
Silence at my side and spoke,
Saying, "You conjecture well:

Yonder is the gate of hell."

Ill as yet the eye could see
The eternal masonry,
But beneath it on the dark
To and fro there stirred a spark.
And again the sombre guide
Knew my question, and replied:
"At hell gate the damned in turn
Pace for sentinel and burn."

Dully at the leaden sky
Staring, and with idle eye
Measuring the listless plain,
I began to think again.
Many things I thought of then,
Battle, and the loves of men,
Cities entered, oceans crossed,
Knowledge gained and virtue lost,
Cureless folly done and said,
And the lovely way that led
To the slimepit and the mire
And the everlasting fire.
And against a smoulder dun
And a dawn without a sun
Did the nearing bastion loom,
And across the gate of gloom
Still one saw the sentry go,
Trim and burning, to and fro,
One for women to admire
In his finery of fire.
Something, as I watched him pace,
Minded me of time and place,
Soldiers of another corps
And a sentry known before.

Ever darker hell on high
Reared its strength upon the sky,
And our footfall on the track
Fetched the daunting echo back.
But the soldier pacing still
The insuperable sill,
Nursing his tormented pride,
Turned his head to neither side,
Sunk into himself apart

And the hell-fire of his heart.
But against our entering in
From the drawbridge Death and Sin
Rose to render key and sword
To their father and their lord.
And the portress foul to see
Lifted up her eyes on me
Smiling, and I made reply:
"Met again, my lass," said I.
Then the sentry turned his head,
Looked, and knew me, and was Ned.

    Once he looked, and halted straight,
Set his back against the gate,
Caught his musket to his chin,
While the hive of hell within
Sent abroad a seething hum
As of towns whose king is come
Leading conquest home from far
And the captives of his war,
And the car of triumph waits,
And they open wide the gates.
But across the entry barred
Straddled the revolted guard,
Weaponed and accoutred well
From the arsenals of hell;
And beside him, sick and white,
Sin to left and Death to right
Turned a countenance of fear
On the flaming mutineer.
Over us the darkness bowed,
And the anger in the cloud
Clenched the lightning for the stroke;
But the traitor musket spoke.

    And the hollowness of hell
Sounded as its master fell,
And the mourning echo rolled
Ruin through his kingdom old.
Tyranny and terror flown
Left a pair of friends alone,
And beneath the nether sky
All that stirred was he and I.

Silent, nothing found to say,
We began the backward way;
And the ebbing luster died
From the soldier at my side,
As in all his spruce attire
Failed the everlasting fire.
Midmost of the homeward track
Once we listened and looked back;
But the city, dusk and mute,
Slept, and there was no pursuit.

XXXII.

When I would muse in boyhood
    The wild green woods among,
And nurse resolves and fancies
    Because the world was young,
It was not foes to conquer,
    Nor sweethearts to be kind,
But it was friends to die for
    That I would seek and find.

I sought them far and found them,
    The sure, the straight, the brave,
The hearts I lost my own to,
    The souls I could not save.
They braced their belts about them,
    They crossed in ships the sea,
They sought and found six feet of ground,
    And there they died for me.

XXXIII.

When the eye of day is shut,
    And the stars deny their beams,
And about the forest hut
    Blows the roaring wood of dreams,

From deep clay, from desert rock,
    From the sunk sands of the main,
Come not at my door to knock,
    Hearts that loved me not again.

Sleep, be still, turn to your rest
    In the lands where you are laid;
In far lodgings east and west
    Lie down on the beds you made.

In gross marl, in blowing dust,
    In the drowned ooze of the sea,
Where you would not, lie you must,
    Lie you must, and not with me.

XXXIV.

THE FIRST OF MAY

The orchards half the way
    From home to Ludlow fair
Flowered on the first of May
    In Mays when I was there;
And seen from stile or turning
    The plume of smoke would show
Where fires were burning
    That went out long ago.

The plum broke forth in green,
    The pear stood high and snowed,
My friends and I between
    Would take the Ludlow road;
Dressed to the nines and drinking
    And light in heart and limb,
And each chap thinking
    The fair was held for him.

Between the trees in flower
    New friends at fairtime tread
The way where Ludlow tower
    Stands planted on the dead.
Our thoughts, a long while after,
    They think, our words they say;
Theirs now's the laughter,
    The fair, the first of May.

Ay, yonder lads are yet
    The fools that we were then;
For oh, the sons we get
    Are still the sons of men.
The sumless tale of sorrow
    Is all unrolled in vain:
May comes to-morrow
    And Ludlow fair again.

XXXV.

When first my way to fair I took
    Few pence in purse had I,
And long I used to stand and look
    At things I could not buy.

Now times are altered: if I care
    To buy a thing, I can;
The pence are here and here's the fair,
    But where's the lost young man?

—To think that two and two are four
    And neither five nor three
The heart of man has long been sore
    And long 'tis like to be.

XXXVI.

REVOLUTION

West and away the wheels of darkness roll,
    Day's beamy banner up the east is borne,
Spectres and fears, the nightmare and her foal,
    Drown in the golden deluge of the morn.

But over sea and continent from sight
    Safe to the Indies has the earth conveyed
The vast and moon-eclipsing cone of night,
    Her towering foolscap of eternal shade.

See, in mid heaven the sun is mounted; hark,
    The belfries tingle to the noonday chime.
'Tis silent, and the subterranean dark
    Has crossed the nadir, and begins to climb.

XXXVII.

EPITAPH ON AN ARMY OF MERCENARIES

These, in the day when heaven was falling,
   The hour when earth's foundations fled,
Followed their mercenary calling
   And took their wages and are dead.

Their shoulders held the sky suspended;
   They stood, and earth's foundations stay;
What God abandoned, these defended,
   And saved the sum of things for pay.

XXXVIII.

Oh stay at home, my lad, and plough
   The land and not the sea,
And leave the soldiers at their drill,
And all about the idle hill
   Shepherd your sheep with me.

Oh stay with company and mirth
   And daylight and the air;
Too full already is the grave
   Of fellows that were good and brave
   And died because they were.

XXXIX.

When summer's end is nighing
   And skies at evening cloud,
I muse on change and fortune
   And all the feats I vowed
   When I was young and proud.

The weathercock at sunset
   Would lose the slanted ray,
And I would climb the beacon
   That looked to Wales away
   And saw the last of day.

From hill and cloud and heaven
    The hues of evening died;
Night welled through lane and hollow
    And hushed the countryside,
    But I had youth and pride.

And I with earth and nightfall
    In converse high would stand,
Late, till the west was ashen
    And darkness hard at hand,
    And the eye lost the land.

The year might age, and cloudy
    The lessening day might close,
But air of other summers
    Breathed from beyond the snows,
    And I had hope of those.

They came and were and are not
    And come no more anew;
And all the years and seasons
    That ever can ensue
    Must now be worse and few.

So here's an end of roaming
    On eves when autumn nighs:
The ear too fondly listens
    For summer's parting sighs,
    And then the heart replies.

XL.

Tell me not here, it needs not saying,
    What tune the enchantress plays
In aftermaths of soft September
    Or under blanching mays,
For she and I were long acquainted
    And I knew all her ways.

On russet floors, by waters idle,
    The pine lets fall its cone;
The cuckoo shouts all day at nothing
    In leafy dells alone;
And traveler's joy beguiles in autumn
    Hearts that have lost their own.

On acres of the seeded grasses
    The changing burnish heaves;
Or marshalled under moons of harvest
    Stand still all night the sheaves;
Or beeches strip in storms for winter
    And stain the wind with leaves.

Possess, as I possessed a season,
    The countries I resign,
Where over elmy plains the highway
    Would mount the hills and shine,
And full of shade the pillared forest
    Would murmur and be mine.

For nature, heartless, witless nature,
    Will neither care nor know
What stranger's feet may find the meadow
    And trespass there and go,
Nor ask amid the dews of morning
    If they are mine or no.

XLI. FANCY'S KNELL

When lads were home from labour
    At Abdon under Clee,
A man would call his neighbor
    And both would send for me.
And where the light in lances
    Across the mead was laid,
There to the dances
    I fetched my flute and played.

Ours were idle pleasures,
    Yet oh, content we were,
The young to wind the measures,
    The old to heed the air;
And I to lift with playing
    From tree and tower and steep
The light delaying,
    And flute the sun to sleep.

The youth toward his fancy
    Would turn his brow of tan,
And Tom would pair with Nancy
    And Dick step off with Fan;
The girl would lift her glances
    To his, and both be mute:
Well went the dances
    At evening to the flute.

Wenlock Edge was umbered,
    And bright was Abdon Burf,
And warm between them slumbered
    The smooth green miles of turf;
Until from grass and clover
    The upshot beam would fade,
And England over
    Advanced the lofty shade.

The lofty shade advances,
    I fetch my flute and play:
Come, lads, and learn the dances
    And praise the tune to-day.
To-morrow, more's the pity,
    Away we both must hie,
To air the ditty,
    And to earth I.

THE END

Made in the USA
Middletown, DE
07 December 2022